W9-DAD-706

Martin Luther King, Jr.

by Jill C. Wheeler

Breaking Barriers

visit us at
www.abdopub.com

Published by ABDO & Daughters, an imprint of ABDO Publishing Company, 4940 Viking Drive, Suite 622, Edina, Minnesota 55435. Copyright ©2003 by Abdo Consulting Group, Inc. International copyrights reserved in all countries. No part of this book may be reproduced in any form without written permission from the publisher.

Printed in the United States.

Edited by Paul Joseph
Graphic Design: John Hamilton
Cover Design: Mighty Media
Interior Photos: AP/Photo, p. 5, 19, 20, 47
Archive Photos, p. 14, 17, 23, 25, 28, 59, 61
Corbis, p. 9, 11, 12, 15, 26, 27, 31, 34, 37, 39, 41, 45, 48, 53, 55, 56, 57, 60
Hulton Getty Archive/Liaison, p. 1, 7, 33, 43, 51

Library of Congress Cataloging-in-Publication Data

Wheeler, Jill C., 1964-
    Martin Luther King, Jr. / Jill C. Wheeler.
        p. cm. — (Breaking barriers)
    Includes index.
    Summary: A biography of the civil rights leader who spent much of his life pursuing his dream of equal treatment for fellow African Americans and for all people.
        ISBN 1-57765-738-1
        1. King, Martin Luther, Jr., 1929-1968—Juvenile literature. 2. African Americans—Biography—Juvenile literature. 3. Civil rights workers—United States—Biography—Juvenile literature. 4. Baptists—United States—Clergy—Biography—Juvenile literature. 5. African Americans—Civil rights—History—20th century—Juvenile literature. [1. King, Martin Luther, Jr., 1929-1968. 2. Civil rights workers. 3. Clergy. 4. Civil rights movements—History. 5. African Americans—Biography.] I. Title.

E185.97.K5 W48 2002
323'.092—dc21
[B]
                                                                2001045084

Contents

The Ghosts Of Birmingham

*I*n April 2001, jurors in Birmingham, Alabama, carefully listened to evidence presented at an unusual trial. The trial was for a crime committed more than 37 years earlier. On Sunday morning, September 15, 1963, a bomb exploded in Birmingham's Sixteenth Street Baptist Church. The dynamite blast destroyed the stately brick church and killed four African-American girls.

The bombing occurred during a time when African-Americans in the southern United States were fighting to end segregation. They wanted to have rights equal to those of white people. Many white southerners did not want to end segregation or give black people equal rights. Some racist white people resorted to violence and terror to stop African-Americans from fighting for their rights.

The Sixteenth Street Baptist Church bombing was just one of many such crimes during those years. But the deaths of four innocent girls made it among the worst. The idea that anyone could murder children while they were at church shocked the nation.

Mourners grieve for one of the victims of the 1963 Birmingham, Alabama, church bombing.

The jury deliberated for a little more than two hours before making a decision. Jurors found 62-year-old Thomas Blanton, Jr., guilty of four counts of first-degree murder. The judge sentenced him to life in prison. Blanton was one of four white men suspected in the bombing of the Sixteenth Street Baptist Church. One was already in prison for the crime, and one had already died. The fourth man had been declared mentally unfit to stand trial.

The trial opened many old wounds for the people of Birmingham. Family members of the four girls were among those who testified. Their stories reminded everyone in the courtroom of the struggle that had plagued many southern cities.

Many people in the community also recalled the funeral service for the girls who died in the bombing. One of the great leaders of the Civil Rights movement gave the eulogy. "They did not die in vain," he said. "The innocent blood of these little girls may well serve as the redemptive force that will bring new light to this dark city."

The speaker was the Reverend Dr. Martin Luther King, Jr. He spent his life working toward his dream of a day when all Americans would live together in peace and brotherhood, regardless of their skin color. Ultimately, he died for this dream.

Martin Luther
King, Jr.

M.L.

*M*artin Luther King, Jr., was born Michael
King, Jr., on January 15, 1929, in Atlanta, Georgia.
His father, Michael King, Sr., worked as the
assistant pastor at Ebenezer Baptist Church. His
mother was Alberta Williams King. Her father
served as the head pastor at Ebenezer Baptist
Church. Alberta had been a teacher before she
married.

Michael King, Sr., changed his son's name to
Martin Luther King, Jr., when the boy was six years
old. Michael King, Sr., changed his own name to
Martin Luther King, as well. The names honored
Martin Luther, the man who sparked the
Protestant Reformation.

Young Martin, or M.L., had an older sister
named Christine. He also had a younger brother
named Alfred Daniel, or A.D.

Martin's grandparents on his father's side were
sharecroppers in rural Georgia. As sharecroppers,
they farmed land that someone else owned and got
part of the profits in return. The landowner received
the other part of the profits.

Ebenezer Baptist Church in Atlanta, Georgia

M.L.'s father knew that he did not want to be a sharecropper when he grew up. So at age 18, Michael left home and moved to Atlanta. He worked during the day and went to school at night. Michael finally earned his high school diploma and then went to Morehouse College to become a minister.

Michael and Alberta married in 1926. They moved in with Alberta's parents, and Michael began assisting his father-in-law at Ebenezer Baptist Church. Michael and Alberta soon started a family. After Alberta's father died, Michael—also known as Daddy King—became the head pastor at Ebenezer Baptist Church. It was an important position. Ebenezer was among the largest African-American churches in Atlanta. Church was an important part of the African-American community. It was one of the few places where African-Americans did not feel the pain of discrimination.

Ebenezer quickly became young Martin's second home. He went to Sunday school every week, and he enjoyed attending both the morning and afternoon worship services. Martin loved the music in church, too. He began singing solos in church when he was only five years old. Whenever he sang, Martin impressed people with his voice. Also by the time Martin was five, he could recite entire Bible passages by heart. And by the time he was six, he knew the words to many hymns from memory.

*Martin Luther King, Sr.,
preaching at Ebenezer
Baptist Church.*

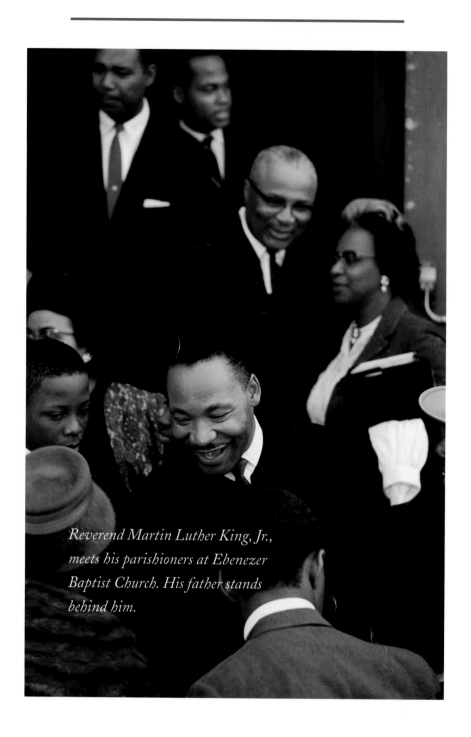

Reverend Martin Luther King, Jr., meets his parishioners at Ebenezer Baptist Church. His father stands behind him.

Martin also enjoyed hearing Daddy King's voice boom from the pulpit. He was proud of the way his father encouraged church members to hold their heads high, even though the white community tried to make them feel ashamed because their skin was dark. Martin was so impressed with sermons he heard by his father and other ministers that he began thinking about becoming a minister himself. He told his parents, "When I grow up, I'm going to get me some big words, too."

At home, Daddy King had a major influence on his family. He was a strict father. His booming voice kept Martin, his brother, and his sister in line. Daddy King also spoke what was on his mind and stood up against discrimination. Once, he and Martin walked out of a shoe store without buying anything because the clerk had refused to serve them in the front of the store. Martin never forgot his father's hatred for segregation. "I don't care how long I have to live with the system," Daddy King said. "I will never accept it."

When he was six, Martin had one of his first experiences with segregation. A white family owned the grocery store across the street from where he lived. Martin often played with their two little boys. One day when he went to ask them to play, their parents came out instead and made excuses about why the boys couldn't come out.

A 1950s bus requiring African-Americans to sit in the rear.

Martin was sad. He told his mother what happened. She took him in her lap and explained to him that their city was segregated. That meant that black people and white people had to stay separate. White people didn't want to share things equally with black people. They had separate churches, separate schools, and separate restaurants. Martin's mother told him about the signs on drinking fountains, restrooms, and waiting rooms that said "Whites Only." Martin later learned that black people could only sit in the backs of the city buses, and he learned just how much the white authorities disrespected and mistreated black people.

This all confused Martin. His father taught him that he should love everyone, white and black people alike. Yet white people were always treating him and his family poorly. "How could I love a race of people who hate me?" he asked himself for many years.

Reverend Martin Luther King, Sr., delivers a sermon from the pulpit at Ebenezer Baptist Church.

Big Words, Big Plans

*D*espite the discrimination of the day, Martin spent his time like many other boys. He enjoyed playing baseball and football, and he liked to ride his bike. Martin was small for his age, but he learned to talk his way out of troublesome situations. When talking didn't work, he wasn't afraid to wrestle. He became known for his wrestling abilities.

Martin's mother had taught him to read at an early age. It was one of his favorite activities. He especially loved reading books about African-American history. He read about African-Americans who had made a difference helping others. He wanted to become one of them. He practiced speeches using the big words he had spoken of as a younger child.

During his junior year in high school, Martin and his teacher traveled to Valdosta, Georgia, for a speech contest. Martin's voice had developed into a deep, rich baritone. His emphatic voice and excellent vocabulary combined to make his speeches outstanding. He earned second prize for his school at the contest.

A young Martin Luther King, Jr.

The successful day was tarnished by the bus ride home from the contest. All the seats were full when a group of white passengers boarded the bus. The white bus driver ordered Martin and his teacher to give up their seats for the white passengers. At first, Martin refused. Then his teacher asked him to give up his seat for her sake. So he did, and they spent the next 90 miles (145 km) back to Atlanta standing. "It was the angriest I have ever been in my life," he recalled later.

Martin was so smart that he skipped both the ninth and twelfth grades. He was ready for college when he was only 15 years old. At this time, the United States was in the middle of World War II. Many young people were serving in the armed forces instead of going to college. So schools, such as Morehouse College in Atlanta, accepted younger students if they could pass the entrance exam. Martin easily passed the test. In the fall of 1944, he enrolled in the all-black college where his father had earned a degree.

Everyone in Martin's family expected him to follow in his father's footsteps and become a minister. They thought it natural for Martin to eventually take over his father's duties at Ebenezer. Martin, however, wasn't so sure that he wanted to be a minister. He did know that he wanted to help people. He considered becoming a doctor or lawyer, because he knew he could help people that way. But he decided instead to major in sociology. He believed the sociology classes would give him a better understanding of people and how they acted.

Martin Luther King, Jr., wasn't sure he wanted to be a minister like his father.

Martin Luther King, Jr.

Martin began thinking more about an essay he had read by Henry David Thoreau. The essay was titled "Civil Disobedience." Thoreau had lived nearly 100 years earlier, but his ideas still had merit. Thoreau said that when laws are unjust, people should refuse to obey them.

Martin began to think that African-Americans might be able to change the unjust segregation laws by refusing to obey them. He decided that many

African-Americans would have to peacefully disobey the laws before anyone would take notice. Therefore, if he were to make a difference, he would have to influence thousands of people. He realized that if he became a minister, he would have that opportunity. Like his father, he could use the pulpit to talk about change and justice.

Martin's desire to change society was magnified even more after the summer of 1945. During that summer, Martin and some of his friends worked in tobacco fields in Connecticut. The work was hard and the days long and hot, but Martin wanted to make enough money to pay for the following year's tuition himself. He didn't want his father to have to pay it as before.

Martin's trip to Connecticut was his first visit to the North. Unlike the South, the North didn't have "Whites Only" signs or segregation laws. Martin enjoyed the freedom of being able to go to any theater he wanted and any restaurant he could afford. Things changed on the train ride home. As soon as the train reached the South, Martin and his friends were sent to a dining table in the rear of the car where the waiter drew a curtain to separate them from the white diners. "I felt as though a curtain had dropped on my selfhood," Martin said of the experience.

Reverend King

*B*y the time Martin was 17 and finishing his junior year at Morehouse, he decided to tell his family about his call to the ministry. He felt more certain than ever that as a minister he could help people with social and spiritual problems. The news delighted Daddy King. He quickly arranged for his son to preach a trial sermon at Ebenezer Baptist Church. After the service, everyone decided that Martin would make an excellent preacher.

Martin was ordained a minister when he was just 19. He was still in college, so he had to continue his studies. At the same time, he became an assistant pastor at Ebenezer. Becoming ordained changed some parts of Martin's life. He had always loved dancing. In fact, he was known as one of the best jitterbug dancers in all of Atlanta. But it was not acceptable for ministers to go to dances. After Martin was ordained, Daddy King found out his son had attended a dance. He made Martin apologize in front of the entire congregation. Martin quickly realized that a minister's personal life is never his own.

Martin graduated from Morehouse College in 1948. He knew he would continue his education, the only question was where.

Reverend Martin Luther King, Jr., in front of the Montgomery, Alabama, state house.

Martin chose Crozer Theological Seminary in Chester, Pennsylvania. Unlike Morehouse, Crozer taught both black and white students. Martin would be one of only six African-American students studying alongside 94 white students.

Martin wanted to prove that he was as capable as any of the white students. He wanted to show them that the stereotypes many white people had about black people were wrong. He stayed up late into the night studying and earned A's in all his courses. He kept his room tidy. He always appeared in clean, pressed clothing, and he always arrived to class on time. Martin also continued to work on the quest that now drove him day and night. He wanted to find a way for African-Americans to achieve equality without force or revolution.

At Crozer, Martin learned about a man named Mahatma Gandhi. Gandhi lived in India when the country was under British rule. The British treated the native Indian people poorly, just as the whites treated the blacks poorly in the South. Gandhi wanted India to gain its independence from Britain. He urged fellow Indians to break unjust laws. When they went to jail because of their disobedience, he told them not to fight back. More and more Indians went to jail under this program. Gandhi called it nonviolent resistance.

Eventually, through Gandhi's nonviolent resistance, India gained its independence. Amazingly, it was a peaceful revolution. Martin wondered if African-Americans could follow a similar path to equality. He didn't know if nonviolent resistance would work, but he knew he wanted to try.

Martin graduated from Crozer Theological Seminary at the top of his class in June 1951. That honor earned him a scholarship to continue his studies. He decided to pursue his doctorate degree at Boston University in Boston, Massachusetts.

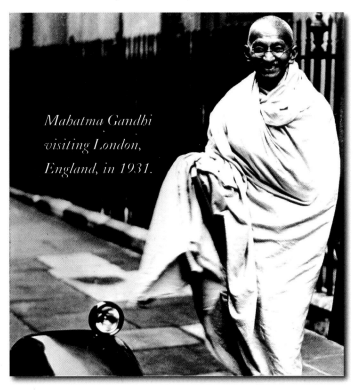

Mahatma Gandhi visiting London, England, in 1931.

Coretta

*B*oston University presented just the kind of atmosphere Martin thrived on. It was a place where people from varying backgrounds gathered. They spent hours discussing life and comparing the works of great philosophers. Martin especially loved to talk about how people could live together in peace. He made many good friends at the university.

One of his friends suggested he meet Coretta Scott, a young woman from Alabama who was attending the New England Conservatory of Music. That school was also in Boston. Coretta had a beautiful voice and was studying to be a professional singer. Martin was intrigued. He called her and arranged to have lunch with her one day.

Coretta Scott King and Martin Luther King, Jr.

Coretta Scott King

Martin Luther King, Jr., and his wife, Coretta Scott King, holding one of their children.

The two spent the entire lunch talking. They shared stories of their pasts, as well as their hopes for the future. Like Martin, Coretta was concerned about the treatment of African-Americans in the South. Her family had been victimized by prejudice many times. When Coretta was growing up, her family's new house suspiciously burned to the ground. The police and fire departments refused to even investigate how the fire had started. Coretta and her family suspected someone had burned it because they didn't think an African-American family should live in such a nice place.

By the end of that first lunch, Martin had already decided he wanted to marry Coretta. The two began spending their spare time together getting to know each other. They often talked about getting married.

The decision to marry Martin was difficult for Coretta. She had planned on a career as a professional singer. She knew she would have to give up that dream if she married Martin. Her career then would be that of a minister's wife. Finally, she decided she loved Martin too much to let him go, and she agreed to marry him.

Coretta and Martin married on June 18, 1953, on the lawn of Coretta's family home in Alabama. Martin's father performed the service. The newlyweds returned to Boston to finish their degrees. Martin completed his classes in August 1953. Now all he had to do was write his Ph.D. dissertation. He decided to take a job while he was working on the paper.

Martin received offers to work at three different colleges. Three churches also expressed interest in hiring him. Two of the churches were in the North. The third was Dexter Avenue Baptist Church in Montgomery, Alabama. Neither Martin nor Coretta were sure if they wanted to return to the segregated South. However, they became convinced that moving back to the South was the right thing to do. They realized they needed to help other African-Americans in their fight for equal rights. "I like this church," Martin said after preaching a trial sermon at Dexter. "This is where I want to begin my ministry."

Back To
The South

*T*he Reverend King started preaching at
Dexter Avenue Baptist Church in May 1954. He
immersed himself in his church work, calling on the
sick, performing weddings and funerals, and
counseling people in need. King's wife finished her
degree the following month. She then joined him to
work as his secretary, and she sang in the church
choir. King spent extra time on his sermons, and soon
word began to spread about the intelligent,
passionate young preacher at Dexter.

As King became more involved in Montgomery's
African-American community, he made many
friends. One was another minister named Ralph
Abernathy. Abernathy became one of Martin's closest
associates. King also joined the local chapter of the
National Association for the Advancement of
Colored People (NAACP). The NAACP was an
organization that worked to improve the lives of
African-Americans.

Martin Luther King, Jr., marches with other religious leaders and activists near Montgomery, Alabama.

In June 1955, King officially received his doctorate degree. That November, he and his wife had a daughter, Yolanda. Life for the family was going smoothly. King, however, was increasingly troubled by the situation he saw in Montgomery.

Montgomery's 50,000 African-Americans were consistently treated as second-class citizens. Virtually every aspect of life in the city was segregated. There were separate churches, schools, and even cemeteries for blacks and whites. The facilities for blacks were never as nice as those for whites. Whites also made it virtually impossible for blacks to vote.

On the surface, life in Montgomery seemed peaceful. Many white people thought their black maids and handymen were content. They could not have been more wrong. As the injustices piled up, the black community became increasingly discontent. Montgomery, like other cities in the South, was like a time bomb that was about to explode.

The explosion began on December 1, 1955. That day, 42-year-old Rosa Parks rode on the city bus after work. All Montgomery city buses were strictly segregated. Blacks had to sit in the rear, and if there were no seats available in the front, white section, blacks had to give up their seats for the whites. Blacks also had to get on the bus at the front, pay the driver, then get off and re-enter at the rear. Many times the bus drove away before they could get back on.

That day, the white section quickly filled up. When more white riders boarded, the bus driver told four passengers in the black section to give up their seats. One of the black passengers was Rosa Parks. While the other three passengers stood up, Parks refused to give up her seat. As she said later, she was tired of giving in to segregation.

Rosa Parks

Martin Luther King, Jr., used the church pulpit to spread his message of civil rights and equality.

The police arrested Parks and took her to jail. Word of the arrest spread quickly through the African-American community. A local leader of the NAACP called King to tell him about the situation. He suggested that African-Americans boycott the bus system in protest. King agreed that was a good idea. He offered Dexter Avenue Church as a meeting place to plan the boycott.

That weekend, King and other community leaders went to work. They prepared leaflets asking African-Americans to stay off the buses that Monday. King and the other black ministers told their congregations about the boycott during Sunday church services. They hoped that telling enough African-Americans about the boycott would make it successful.

On Monday morning, the Kings anxiously watched the bus stop outside their home. Buses began to roll by, but there were no blacks riding on them. Instead, blacks walked to work, shared rides, or even rode in horse-drawn carts. The boycott was a success.

King and the other African-American community leaders decided to extend the boycott until the Montgomery bus company agreed to treat black passengers with more respect. To accomplish this, they formed the Montgomery Improvement Association (MIA). They elected King president.

The boycott stretched on, and the tension increased. The white community did everything it could to stop the boycott. White police officers arrested black taxi drivers who were taking people to work for the same price as the bus. They arrested volunteer drivers for the smallest violation or, sometimes, for no violation at all. King himself was arrested while driving a car pool. The police officer said he had been speeding even though he had not.

The hatred followed King home, as well. He received 30 to 40 hate letters and obscene phone calls a day. The writers and callers called him names and threatened his life. They disliked the work he was doing to gain equal civil rights for black people.

The tension and fear increased further on January 30, 1956. King was speaking at a meeting while his wife and baby Yolanda were at home with a friend. They heard a thump on their front porch and ran to the back of the house just as a bomb exploded. The blast split the front porch in two and showered the living room with broken glass.

When King found out he rushed home. By the time he arrived, a crowd of angry blacks had gathered at the house. The white police arrived and tried unsuccessfully to break up the crowd. King feared the crowd would become violent. "If you have weapons, take them home," he said. "If you do not have them, please do not seek to get them. We cannot solve this problem through retaliatory violence... . We must meet hate with love."

The crowd listened to King in amazement. Here was a man whose home had just been bombed, and he was telling them not to fight back. This was the first true test of King's commitment to peaceful, nonviolent resistance.

Police arrest Martin Luther King, Jr., in Montgomery, Alabama.

Warrior For Peace

The Montgomery bus boycott went on for more than a year. In November 1956, the U.S. Supreme Court ruled that segregation in the bus system was unconstitutional. The following month, the city of Montgomery was forced to treat blacks and whites equally on city buses.

African-Americans throughout the South cheered at the victory in Montgomery. Many thought that if they could defeat segregation on the buses, they could defeat it in other areas of their lives.

King joined with a group of black ministers from around the South to continue the fight against segregation. They formed the Southern Christian Leadership Conference (SCLC). They elected King president of the organization.

Martin Luther King, Jr., speaks at a civil rights rally in Canton, Mississippi.

King made speech after speech to African-Americans throughout the South. Like Gandhi, King urged them to disobey unjust laws. King said that if they were arrested they should cooperate with the police and go to jail quietly. He believed that whites would eventually get tired of arresting people who didn't fight back. "We must have the courage to refuse to fight back," he told them. "We must use the weapon of love."

In 1958, King and the SCLC focused on registering blacks to vote. That fall, King also promoted a book he had written about the Montgomery bus boycott. While promoting the book in New York City, a disturbed woman stabbed him with a razor-sharp letter opener. The blade just missed his heart. His doctor said that if he had as much as sneezed, he would have died.

The following winter, King, his wife, and a friend traveled to India to learn more about the legacy of Gandhi. King returned from India with an even better understanding of the power of nonviolence. He also found himself even more committed to using it through the SCLC. While King enjoyed working at Dexter Avenue Baptist Church, he resigned to join his father as co-pastor at Ebenezer Baptist Church in Atlanta. That way he would have more time to devote to the peaceful fight for freedom.

Martin Luther King, Jr., meets parishioners at Ebenezer Baptist Church after Sunday services.

Martin Luther King, Jr.

"We Shall Overcome"

*B*ack in Atlanta, King continued to preach his message of nonviolent resistance. Tens of thousands of people listened. In 1960, they began sit-ins at whites-only lunch counters. Each day, blacks and even some supportive whites would go to the counters and ask to be served. They would sit quietly even though they were refused service and teased or even beaten.

Other activists became Freedom Riders. They were blacks and whites who joined together to end segregation. Freedom Riders rode on buses in the South and sat in whites-only bus stations and waiting rooms to protest the unjust laws. Angry whites set some of the buses on fire and attacked the riders. Police arrested thousands of other riders and put them in jail. Many sang an old Negro spiritual titled "We Shall Overcome" as police led them off. The song quickly became the anthem of the Civil Rights movement. King joined those doing sit-ins and Freedom Riders in their protests.

Martin Luther King, Jr., speaks at a civil rights rally.

King's activities left him little time to spend with his family. His second child, Martin Luther King III, had been born in October 1957, and his third child, Dexter, had been born in January 1961. Another daughter, Bernice, was born in March 1963. Even though King was usually away from home, he made sure to call his family every night to ask them about their day. He also tried to be home every Sunday for dinner, and to be present for every child's birthday.

Times were difficult for King's children, too. Like their father, they were often criticized, especially by other children. And they themselves also found it hard to understand why their father was in jail so frequently. "He went to jail to help people," their mother would explain to them.

Battle In Birmingham

*I*n 1963, King and the SCLC decided next to focus their attention on Birmingham, Alabama. Most people regarded Birmingham as the most segregated city in the South. Birmingham officials firmly opposed desegregation.

King knew the only chance for success would come from many, many protesters. He would need thousands of activists to get Birmingham to change its ways. The struggle began with sit-ins and protest marches. As expected, Birmingham police officers arrested many people.

Then King and the other leaders had an idea. They planned a protest march for children. King knew all too well how much segregation hurt children. It pained him to have to tell his own children that there were places they couldn't go simply because they were black.

More than 2,500 children turned out for the march. Unbelievably, Birmingham police officers responded with violence. They opened up fire hoses on the marchers, and the force of the water knocked them to the ground. Then they unleashed their dogs on the helpless children. Television crews captured the entire scene. Millions of people around the nation were shocked and horrified when they watched the news and saw children being hurt.

The protests and violence in Birmingham raged for more than a month. Finally, the city leaders agreed to desegregate lunch counters, restrooms, and drinking fountains. The city leaders also agreed to hire some African-Americans and work toward better race relations.

Three demonstrators join hands against the force of water sprayed by riot police in Birmingham, Alabama.

"I Have A Dream"

*K*ing believed the cause of freedom had won a
solid victory in Birmingham. He thought that blacks
were making progress, and he wanted to organize
even more nonviolent protests in other cities. The
U.S. Congress was now considering passing
significant civil rights legislation. To help the
legislation pass, King and other SCLC members
began planning a march on the nation's capital,
Washington, D.C.

The march took place on August 28, 1963. More
than 250,000 people of all ages and races gathered in
front of the Lincoln Memorial. They listened quietly
and peacefully as speaker after speaker addressed
them. Finally it was King's turn. "I have a dream," he
said, "that one day on the red hills of Georgia, the
sons of former slaves and the sons of former slave-
owners will be able to sit down together at the table
of brotherhood."

Martin Luther King, Jr., acknowledges the crowd at the Lincoln Memorial for his "I Have a Dream" speech during the March on Washington, D.C., on August 28, 1963.

*Martin Luther King, Jr., holds his son
Dexter on his lap at his home in
Atlanta, Georgia. That day, King was
informed that he would receive the
1964 Nobel Peace Prize.*

The crowd was inspired as King outlined his dream for the future. Thousands cried as he finished his speech with the words of an old Negro spiritual, "Free at last! Free at last! Thank God Almighty, we are free at last!"

The march was the largest ever held in Washington, D.C. It quickly called attention to the importance of civil rights legislation. President Lyndon Johnson signed the Civil Rights Act into law in the summer of 1964. King was there to witness the signing. The act was the most far-reaching civil rights legislation since right after the U.S. Civil War.

The march on Washington helped land King on the cover of *Time* magazine as Man of the Year in 1963. The following year, King received an even bigger honor. He was selected to receive the Nobel Peace Prize. At age 35, he became the youngest person ever to win the international award. He accepted the award in the name of all the people who had contributed to the fight for freedom.

The March To Selma

*T*he new Civil Rights Act went a long way toward ending segregation in the South. However, it still was difficult for blacks to register to vote. White voting officials often wouldn't announce when the registration office would be open. Or, when blacks arrived to register, officials would tell them that the office was closing.

This was especially true in Selma, Alabama. The city's population was 50 percent black, but 99 percent of its registered voters were white. The SCLC chose Selma as the place to hold a march to draw attention to voting rights issues.

In March 1965, a group of 500 demonstrators set out from Selma to the state capitol building in Montgomery. Alabama state troopers quickly met them and ordered them to go back. When the marchers refused, the troopers attacked them with clubs and tear gas.

Several days later, King attempted another Selma-to-Montgomery march. Once again, troopers met the protesters just outside town. King turned the protesters back to avoid another violent confrontation. They tried

Martin Luther King, Jr., gives a speech at a church in Selma, Alabama.

again in another week, and this time they were successful. Three hundred demonstrators walked the 54 miles (87 km) to Montgomery to protest voter registration policies. A total of 50,000 people gathered for the march's conclusion.

The Selma march called national attention to the problem. Soon after that, Congress passed the Voting Rights Act. Federal officials quickly went to work registering black voters. The victory came at a price, though. White racists murdered two white activists who had come to help with the march.

The Movement Stumbles

By 1965, King had helped African-Americans throughout the South defeat segregation laws. He had also helped secure passage of legislation that ensured that all blacks could vote. Now he turned his attention north to Chicago, Illinois.

African-Americans in the North didn't have to fight obvious segregation laws, but they still faced discrimination. Many landlords would not rent to blacks. Often, the only places blacks could live were in dirty, rat-infested apartments called slums. King and his family moved to Chicago to help blacks win the right to better housing. The King family even lived in the slums themselves to call attention to the problem. They were successful in getting city leaders to agree that landlords had to rent to blacks and whites alike.

The Civil Rights movement under King's leadership was slowly moving forward. But all of this progress didn't come quickly enough for some people. Around the nation, many blacks were beginning to believe that King's nonviolent protests weren't changing things fast enough. Other black leaders said that blacks should fight back.

King understood why some people felt that way. But he feared that fighting violence with more violence would only make things worse. "Let us not despair," he said. "Let us not lose faith in man and certainly not in God."

King, still believing in nonviolent protests, began to plan another march on Washington. This one would be a march for poor people. It would call attention to the problem of poverty in the United States among blacks and whites alike.

Dr. Martin Luther King, Jr., ducks after being hit on the head by a rock during a housing discrimination protest in Chicago. Spectators threw rocks, bottles, and firecrackers at the marchers.

Memphis

*I*n the spring of 1968, while King was planning the Poor People's March, he received a call from garbage collectors in Memphis. The Memphis garbage collectors union was on strike. The black garbage collectors were tired of poor working conditions. They were getting nowhere in their negotiations with the city. They hoped King could help them.

King agreed to lead a march in Memphis. He was leading 6,000 people in a peaceful march when something went horribly wrong. A group of angry young people who did not believe in nonviolence began smashing windows. King quickly called off the march. He was hurt that people were beginning to turn away from his methods. He wanted to try the march in Memphis one more time.

King returned to Memphis on April 3. That night, he spoke at a rally of supporters. "I've been to the mountaintop," he said. "And I've seen the promised land. I may not get there with you. But... we as a people will get to the promised land."

Dr. Martin Luther King, Jr., speaks to supporters in Memphis, Tennessee, the night before his assassination.

On April 4, King spent the day planning the march. That evening, he stepped out onto the balcony of his motel before dinner. Suddenly, a sound like a firecracker rang out and King crumpled to the floor. His friend Ralph Abernathy raced to his side and saw that he had been shot in the neck. Within an hour, King was dead.

Less than a year later, James Earl Ray pleaded guilty to King's murder. Ray was a racist white man and a convicted criminal. The judge sentenced him to 99 years in prison.

James Earl Ray, seen here being led to court, was convicted of killing Martin Luther King, Jr.

A sign and wreath mark the site where Martin Luther King, Jr., was assassinated at the Lorraine Hotel in Memphis, Tennessee, in 1968.

MARTIN LUTHER KING, JR
JAN 15, 1929 —— APR 4, 1968
FOUNDING PRESIDENT
SOUTHERN CHRISTIAN LEADERSHIP CONFERENCE
THEY SAID ONE TO ANOTHER
BEHOLD HERE COMETH THE DREAMER
LET US SLAY HIM
AND WE SHALL SEE WHAT WILL BECOME OF HIS DREAMS
GENESIS 37 19 - 20
RALPH DAVID ABERNATHY, PRESIDENT

A Nation Mourns

*P*resident Johnson declared April 7 a national day of mourning. Funeral services were held for the Reverend Dr. Martin Luther King, Jr., on April 9, 1968. Abernathy gave the eulogy at the funeral at Ebenezer Baptist Church. It was the very place King had grown up, been ordained, preached, and served as co-pastor with his father. He was buried in Atlanta, Georgia.

In 1983, the U.S. Congress created a national holiday honoring King. The holiday falls on the third Monday in January, near King's January 15 birthday.

Coretta Scott King has kept her husband's dream alive. She was instrumental in opening the Martin Luther King, Jr., Center for Nonviolent Social Change in Atlanta, Georgia.

Reverend Dr. Martin Luther King, Jr.

Timeline

1929: Martin Luther King, Jr., is born January 15 in Atlanta, Georgia.

1953: King marries Coretta Scott on June 18.

1954: King becomes a pastor at Dexter Avenue Baptist Church.

1955: King receives his doctorate degree. Local leaders elect King president of the Montgomery Improvement Association (MIA).

1957: The Southern Christian Leadership Conference (SCLC) begins civil rights work with King as president.

1963: King gives his "I Have a Dream" speech to marchers in Washington, D.C.

1964: King receives the Nobel Peace Prize. President Lyndon Johnson signs the Civil Rights Act.

1965: Protesters march from Selma to Montgomery to draw attention to voter registration problems. Congress passes the Voting Rights Act.

1968: King is assassinated on April 4.

1983: Congress creates a national holiday to honor King and the movement he led.

Web Sites

Would you like to learn more about Martin Luther King, Jr.? Please visit **www.abdopub.com** to find up-to-date Web site links about Martin Luther King, Jr., and the Civil Rights movement. These links are routinely monitored and updated to provide the most current information available.

Martin Luther King, Jr., delivers his "I Have a Dream" speech August 28, 1963, in Washington, D.C.

Glossary

activist

A person who works for political change.

boycott

To refrain from having any dealings with something in order to make a point or change a condition.

Civil Rights movement

The struggle to gain full citizenship rights for African-Americans.

congregation

An assembly of people meeting for religious instruction.

discriminate

To act on a prejudice, such as a racial prejudice.

eulogy

A speech in memory of someone, usually at his or her funeral.

negro spirituals
Religious songs that African-American slaves sang.

Nobel Peace Prize
An annual prize recognizing someone who has worked for peace.

ordain
To be officially appointed a minister.

Protestant Reformation
A religious revolution in the Christian church, which resulted in the start of Protestant churches.

pulpit
A stage or platform used for preaching.

seminary
A school for training priests, ministers, or rabbis.

testify
To make a statement in a trial based on personal knowledge.

unconstitutional
Something that goes against the laws of the U.S. Constitution.

Index

JB
King

Wheeler, Jill C.
Martin Luther King, Jr